SERVICE LEARNING FOR TEENS™

WORKING WITH IMMIGRANTS AND MIGRANT POPULATIONS THROUGH SERVICE LEARNING

MARY BLOUNT CHRISTIAN

ROSEN PUBLISHING®

New York

Published in 2015 by The Rosen Publishing Group, Inc.
29 East 21st Street, New York, NY 10010

Copyright © 2015 by The Rosen Publishing Group, Inc.

First Edition

All rights reserved. No part of this book may be reproduced in any form
without permission in writing from the publisher, except by a reviewer.

Library of Congress Cataloging-in-Publication Data

Christian, Mary Blount.
Working with immigrants and migrant populations through service learning/
Mary Blount Christian.
     pages cm.—(Service learning for teens)
Includes bibliographical references and index.
ISBN 978-1-4777-7969-9 (library bound)
1. Social work with immigrants—United States—Juvenile literature. 2.
Service learning—United States—Juvenile literature. I. Title.
HV4010.C47 2015
362.89'9125307155—dc23

                                                          2014009015

Manufactured in the United States of America

CONTENTS

INTRODUCTION

There are ample opportunities to bond with immigrant or migrant students at your school during the day. Many may not be able to participate in after-school activities, though, because they work alongside their families.

I magine that you look around you, and nothing is familiar. The buildings tower above you, and the people are dressed differently and speak words you do not know. Signs are everywhere: Do Not Walk; Danger, High Voltage; and Do Not Enter, but you cannot read them.

Now imagine a friendly smile, an extended hand, and someone asking in your own language, "May I help you?" You could be that helping hand by creating or participating in a service-learning project that helps immigrant or migrant communities. Service learning is different than traditional volunteering. Through service learning, students apply lessons they learned in a classroom to service projects in the community where they see the principles of civic responsibility in practice. The goal is to enhance the education process through practical experience.

Immigrant children, especially those with migrant parents, are always "the new kid in school." They may feel especially out of place as circumstances keep them from bonding activities like after-school games and rallies.

Angie is a greeter. She gives out bilingual information and school maps to a new student. She tries to match him to a language student with similar interests who will be his lunch buddy and guide until he adjusts.

"I know how he feels," she said. "It's tough coming here mid-semester. You feel as if you're always running to catch up."

This service-learning project didn't begin there. It took social studies classes to investigate the challenge of helping immigrant students, language classes to translate their solutions, and then art and computer classes to create and produce pamphlets. It took area businesses to voluntarily donate supplies and to print the materials.

By the time you complete high school, you will be near voting age. But you needn't wait to make a vital impact on your community. When young people speak as a group, people listen. "Conscientization" is a conscious awareness of social challenges that create one's need to change them. It is a word used by Paulo Freier, a Brazilian educator and philosopher from the last century, in speaking about cultural injustices. It sums up the first two steps in service-learning principles: identify goals and apply skills and knowledge from the core curriculum toward a community need.

With partners like community leaders, educators, families, businesses, organizations, and other youth, students address a specific need. The project may be tutoring adults or younger children or conducting forums and exhibits that bring diverse cultures together to solve mutual needs. It may be reading bilingual books to toddlers or writing letters to area representatives. It could be supporting immigrants on their path to citizenship.

Service learning gives youth a voice and provides leadership opportunities to change the world for the better. Many students discover their futures in careers that begin with recognizing a need in their communities. In their quests for solutions, they find themselves.

CHAPTER ONE

A NATION OF IMMIGRANTS

The United States is a nation of immigrants. It is the most culturally diverse nation in the world. Whether they refer to the United States as États-Unis, Vereinigte Staaten, Stati Uniti, or simply as el Norte, to the foreign-born, the United States usually means the promise of financial, physical, and emotional security.

According to the Congressional Budget Office, one of every eight persons living in the United States today is an immigrant, meaning that they are foreign born. They represent nearly fifty different cultures from Western Europe, Eastern Europe, Asia, the Middle East, and Latin countries, among others.

Each culture brings with it a language and traditions in courtship, marriage, childrearing, faith, and family values that may be at odds with the established culture. They also bring a rich history and memories to share with those who would listen.

Students looking for service-learning projects may find easier ones, but they will find none with more impact on individuals and their community than those partnering with the diverse cultures among them.

FROM BLENDER TO STEW POT

Through the early twentieth century, many new immigrants to the United States set aside their native customs and cultures to assimilate to become what was perceived as "American." That version of "American" was largely defined by the earliest European settlers in the United States. However, as time passed, each group's differences from others seemed to disappear or become less central. People referred to the United States as a "melting pot."

Today, immigrants are more likely to retain their ethnic customs and beliefs, even their manner of dress. The United States is now referred to as a "stew pot," a "salad bowl," or a "mosaic." That is, each culture remains distinctive and recognizable among the population. Many immigrants tend to seek out others of similar backgrounds, forming ethnic communities within cities and towns. Areas with shops and eateries with ethnic foods and signs in foreign languages can be tourist attractions, but to the ethnic groups, they are a little bit of home.

MELTING AWAY MISUNDERSTANDINGS

Differences often isolate cultures and bring about distrust and misconceptions in communities. However, students can create and perform service-learning projects that humanize the challenges of cultural diversity.

Service learning does not always have to happen in person. You can correspond with immigrant or migrant students in other places through e-mail, Skype, social media, and other online tools.

Projects involving immigrants are not limited to topics related to civics or social studies classes. Students interested in virtually any subject from physical education to language arts, history, and journalism may adopt projects or design their own to meet the challenges inherent in cultural diversity.

"I thought all Caucasian kids were *fresas* [snobs]," Lupe said. That was until high school students in Humble, Texas, near Houston, became cyber pen pals with English as a Second Language (ESL) students across town. The advanced language class wrote their notes in Spanish, and the ESL students replied in English. Together they planned a Mexican wedding as part of the curriculum. They also learned a lot about negotiation and compromise, budgeting, and planning ahead, even anticipating potential problems.

"It was really cool connecting with a younger student from a completely different background," one high school student told his teacher.

Near the end of the school year, the classes got together for the mock wedding and reception. "I felt like we helped each other, and just kept watching him get into what we were doing really felt good," the Humble student said, according to the Service Learning Texas website.

The Internet and programs like Skype allow participants to reach beyond their immediate areas. Students report mutual benefits when diverse cultures come together for common causes. Projects with modest goals produce a bigger impact than the participants first imagined.

"I was only a 15-year-old sophomore [at Fieldston School in the Bronx, NY]," Chelsea Dale, creator of the On Giants' Shoulders project, said. Even through college, she continued her successful project to motivate minority children at risk of dropping out of school. Dale hopes to set up branches of her outreach project in the United States and eventually in other countries.

WHY DO THEY COME?

Not all immigrants seek permanent residence for the same reasons. They come for family, better employment opportunities, or humanitarian reasons. Family members of those already living in the United States get priority. Next are those who are highly skilled professionals.

American companies often hire foreign professionals in science, technology, engineering, and mathematics fields when they can't find enough qualified employees locally. The children of these professionals may find assimilation more difficult. Projects like Mix It Up, sponsored by Teaching Tolerance, encourage lunch breaks where students from diverse backgrounds socialize and examine and discuss social boundaries with each other.

Refugees are individuals who fled their home countries because they faced persecution or other dangerous conditions. Refugees already living in the

Students can use lunch breaks to socialize with peers of different backgrounds in a more relaxed environment. They will discover that they share many common interests, goals, and challenges.

United States who believe their lives are in danger have a year to prove that returning to their homeland is lethal. If they are successful, they become asylees. They may be the least prepared for life in the United States. A Colorado Springs, Colorado, newspaper reported a waiting list of immigrants needing English tutors, for instance.

One group of students, in partnership with local organizations, helped locate affordable housing, filled the pantry and fridge with familiar food, donated furnishings, and prepared a booklet of helpful information. Their class studied the culture to learn food taboos and located grocers that stocked ethnic ingredients.

By learning about the countries of origin of those they work with, students can learn about cultural food preferences and taboos. A well-stocked kitchen and a directory of area shops and services can make immigrants feel more at home.

Projects that shed prejudice and distrust may be as simple as breaking bread together or as involved as organizing a traveling display of mementoes from countries of origin. Students can also trace their families' immigration journeys using colored yarn on a world map. Open house displays at a school or public venue can draw parents and initiate dialogue about common experiences and cultural pride. Encouraging parents to share their rich histories gets whole families involved in the education and exchange process.

THE INVITED GUESTS

Not all businesses look for highly skilled workers. Nor do they seek permanent workers. "Guest workers" get temporary visas to supplement resort staffs during peak seasons or to follow the planting and harvest seasons throughout the country. Workers who follow planting and harvest work are usually referred to as migrants. Domestic help may be paid by the room, and seasonal farmworkers may be paid by the bucket instead of an hourly wage, according to the United Farmworkers of America.

The spouses and children of "guest workers" cannot legally work, yet they often toil for free alongside paid workers to help produce more. Language students will find service-learning projects as partners to migrant health clinics. Reading to or playing games with young children in the waiting areas and assisting in securing records of vaccinations are only two of the possibilities.

THE VIEW FROM WASHINGTON

"I believe in the idea of amnesty for those who have put down roots and lived here, even though some time back they may have entered illegally," President Ronald Reagan said in 1984, according to NPR.

In a July 4th speech in 2012 President Barack Obama said, "One lesson of these 236 years is clear—immigration makes America stronger. Immigration makes us stronger. And immigration positions America to lead in the twenty-first century."

In a speech in November 2013, former Secretary of State Hillary Rodham Clinton said, "Our diversity is one of our great strengths, and part of the obvious argument for immigration reform is that we are a country of immigrants, and we should be celebrating that rather than fearing it."

Immigration policies change with administrations and labor needs. In 1882 the federal government passed the first significant immigration law, the Chinese Exclusion Act, which prohibited Chinese immigrants—many of whom were laborers—from entering the United States. For the next ten years individual states regulated immigration.

Ellis Island, the first federal immigration station, opened January 1, 1892. Annie Moore, a teenager from County Cork, Ireland, was the first immigrant processed there. In 1965 new laws ended the quota system that favored immigrants from Europe and since, immigrants from many countries have come to the United States. However, there are still many issues related to immigration that lawmakers must contend with.

Children often join their farmworker parents before and after school. They average sixteen to eighteen hours a week in the fields. Migrant children may be in as many as three different schools in one year. They are always "the new kid in class."

Migrant children have little time or energy for schoolwork. Dropout rates are estimated from 60 to 90 percent by the United Farmworkers of America.

Language students can help migrant workers with vaccination records at an area health clinic. Complete permanent records of inoculations are usually required for admission into schools and will help workers and their families avoid duplicate vaccinations.

Service-learning participants, with partners like Student Action with Farmworkers, assemble facts specific to their communities. They work to eradicate the challenges their classmates face. Through *intercambio* (mutual language exchange), they teach each other about language and culture and work for change.

The greatest need for service-learning projects lies with the large number of Spanish-speaking immigrants. According to the U.S. Census Bureau, one out of every five immigrants living in the United States is from Mexico, South America, or another part of Latin America. They represent the greatest number of under-educated and low-skilled workers.

According to the Census Bureau data nearly two-thirds of the 5.4 million legal immigrants from Mexico have been in the United States long enough to qualify for naturalization. A survey by the Pew Hispanic Center found that only 36 percent apply.

This speaks to the need for service-learning projects to tutor eligible adults and children age fifteen or older in English, and to help them prepare for the U.S. Naturalization test.

HIDING IN PLAIN SIGHT

Eleven million Spanish-speaking immigrants have either entered the United States without documents or simply vanished into the general population when their temporary visas expired. They are considered illegal—that is, they have no green cards (legal documents) giving them the right to live and work in the United States. The Farmworkers of America

estimates that 80 to 90 percent of seasonal farmworkers may be illegal.

The Pew Hispanic Center estimated that in 2010,
4.5 million children born in the United States (U.S.
citizens) had at least one parent who was an unauthorized immigrant. Their siblings may have been brought
to the United States as infants and not even know
their immigration status until they apply for a driver's
license or a college loan.

DREAM OR NIGHTMARE

Seventy-five percent of citizens support a path to citizenship for unauthorized immigrants. Congress has
yet to agree upon that path.

Here may be where service learning can have the
greatest impact for both students and communities.
Public service announcements, newspaper articles,
and neighborhood forums and town halls with students presenting facts can help bring misunderstand-
ings to the surface.

The children who were brought to America by their
undocumented parents have the most uncertain futures
of all. They grow up American. They go through the
school system, speak English, and dream of becoming
doctors, scientists, or serving in the armed forces. They
are called "Dreamers."

The Deferred Action for Childhood Arrivals (DACA)
program temporarily allows those between fifteen and
thirty years of age at the time the bill was enacted to
remain in the United States without fear of deportation. According to U.S. Citizenship and Immigration

Town hall–style meetings in neighborhoods and schools allow students to ask questions and promote discussion about policies that may benefit immigrants and migrants who may be too afraid to come forward or who may lack the means to do so.

Services, only a little more than half of those eligible for deferred action have applied since its inception. Many cite fear of being turned down and arrested for deportation.

Reva excelled in her courses and qualified to be a registered nurse, but she cannot get a license. "I return home after work," Reva (a pseudonym) said. "I cannot breathe until I see Mama in the kitchen preparing the meal like always." Like many others, she fears discovering that her parent is one of the 1,300 arrested and deported to the border every day.

Renaldo (a pseudonym) earned his degree in engineering. Instead of building bridges and dams, he is a carpenter. There are many similar stories. They are united by one word: fear.

Service-learning students, in concert with their civics, social studies, and other classes, find films like *The Dream Is Now*, about undocumented immigrant youth, helpful in starting a community dialogue. It is available free for download on the web.

Middle and high school students will find the subject rich in potential projects for community impact. Look around your classroom, school, and community. Make note of what you observe. The flipside of challenge is solution, and no one is more capable of finding those solutions than young people who follow the principles of service learning.

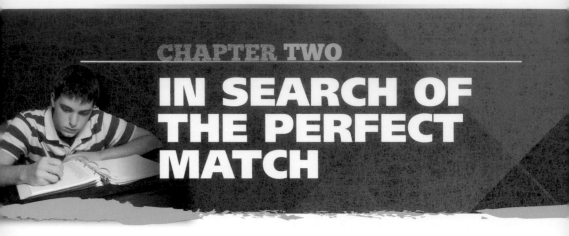

CHAPTER TWO

IN SEARCH OF THE PERFECT MATCH

Service learning combines classroom learning with serving concrete needs in a community. Some school districts have yet to adopt service learning. For others, eighty hours of service learning is mandatory for graduation. The hours required in service are usually twenty hours per semester, freshman through senior years. The balance varies, but it appears that most students divide the hours between class time and actual service.

Service-learning tenets are simple and straight-forward:

- Investigate and analyze the community's needs
- Prepare through curriculum and sponsor resources
- Take action in the time agreed upon
- Reflect on the reciprocal results
- Celebrate through public acknowledgement to inspire others

The first step is to investigate and analyze the community's needs. Some immigrant communities are predominantly Spanish speaking. Others are largely

African or Asian. Ethnicity determines the challenges students face.

Preparation includes consulting with the target communities as well as agencies and organizations interested in partnering with them and with you. The National Service-Learning Clearinghouse (NSLC) is part of Learn and Serve America (a branch of the federal government's Corporation for National Service). Its website offers thousands of free online resources, a large library of service-learning materials, and reference and technical assistance.

Sponsors, administrators, and students agree on a time frame that works for all of them. Some projects may extend beyond a semester and need more than a single sponsor.

Service learners reflect on their experiences periodically and at the conclusion of the project. Hindsight is a valuable tool when designing a new project or regrouping to continue an ongoing project.

Celebrating through public acknowledgement inspires others. It not only leads the way for the next service learners but also acknowledges the students' successes and the benefits gained by communities served.

There are two types of service learning, direct and indirect. Direct service entails working directly with others: for example, being a mentor or tutor for ESL students or adults. Indirect service includes conducting fund-raisers or drives for food or clothing, or in advocacy to right an injustice. The latter may also include letter writing, lobbying the local or national government, or producing public service announcements, town hall meetings, or exhibits to inform the community.

Sponsoring a drive for usable clothing and linens is an example of indirect service learning. Even if students don't interact directly with those who benefit from the drive, the service is no less important.

Service learning has become an important part in practicing citizenship, leadership, and giving youth a voice in their future.

DIFFERENT DRUM BEATS

Because some of us thrive better in groups while others prefer working solo, some districts sponsor individual service-learning projects as well as class or school-wide projects. Some needs in communities are better met by individuals. A horde of volunteers can overwhelm small organizations.

Volunteer Match Organization keeps tabs on needs in areas around the country, and many of these are opportunities for individual volunteers. Enter your town on the website to see a list of needs. A good source for online information is the service project tool kit "Youth Changing the World," which is produced by Youth Service America in cooperation with its numerous big-name sponsors. It is a step-by-step guide with questions that keep you focused on your plan. It works for groups and for individuals.

Malibu High School in California recommends projects with approved area associations on its website: Para Los Niños, with its need for reading tutors, or Juan Cabrillo After School Project, are two that involve the immigrant community.

Baltimore City Public Schools in Maryland and schools in Rochester, New York, allow individual projects that meet the same criteria as group-based projects. The service learner will need a sign-off on hours served and an assessment of success by the agency.

The Chicago school system lists 250 agencies with needs including Asian Health Coalition of Illinois, Aspira of Illinois, and Chinese Mutual Aid Society, all of which support Chicago's refugee and immigrant community. Check out your city's directory for agencies, organizations, associations, and societies if your district doesn't already have an approved list. Compiling a list and interviewing the agencies regarding their needs is a valid service-learning project, too.

IN GOOD COMPANY

Your teacher will generally have a lot of input on what projects you pursue, but most projects begin with studying the changes in immigration policy in the past and their impact. Follow-up investigation includes examining media reports and having a class discussion on the implications of current local proposals and those in Congress, and then thinking about how the class might impact the immigrant community in a positive way.

Your history or social studies class will identify some of the challenges immigrant communities face. For instance, investigation shows that up to 90 percent of adult immigrants want to be citizens, but they are not applying. Why? Many students volunteer to research online and with community associations to find out.

Or perhaps you live in one of at least a dozen states or in the District of Columbia, where the undocumented may obtain driver's licenses. Statistics show that many still drive illegally.

You discover that the citizenship and most drivers' tests require a working knowledge of English. Several students advocate a project to prepare unlicensed drivers for the written test. A committee will investigate what that requires of you and your classmates. A class member suggests it may be better to help the undocumented become legal. That, too, requires oral and written English.

Surveying previous projects through the National Service-Learning Clearinghouse uncovered a world studies class in Chicago that, with training and supervision from local lawyers, helped 200 people file their necessary documents.

DIVIDE TO CONQUER

In a classroom of twenty-eight students, you probably have dozens of suggestions for a project. When

Children may not be the only ones who need tutoring. In most states, applicants for citizenship or driving tests must know not only the correct answers but also how to answer them in English.

deciding which projects to work on, it may help to divide the class into teams to research and present the pros and cons.

Do you want to work with the next generation as mentors, or work with adults to become fully functioning citizens? The pro-contemporary or younger students group suggests that it could be fun, and it could happen mostly during school hours. It probably wouldn't require many supplies, either—a plus. Their school could be the sponsor, another hurdle avoided.

The pro-adult group reminds you that it seems like a two-part project. First, you must tutor in English, and then on the information they must know for citizenship. This is a great project to start as freshmen and follow through the high school years. It may be a bit complicated later. It may even include a semester of bonding and building trust. You have logistics to consider and funds to raise. It requires an early start and training by experts.

Download the booklet "Helping Immigrants Become New Americans: Communities Discuss the Issues," prepared by the Office of Citizenship in the U.S. Citizenship and Immigration Services. With some training, student volunteers may be able to help. Some of the projects can be costly in both money and time. Just how committed are you?

TAKE A GOOD LOOK

How much time are you willing to give? There's no guarantee that any project takes only the required time. Are you organized? You must get accurate and complete records from your initial thoughts through to the final publication of your project. Your insights, impressions, and observations on every phase of the project are vital. You will probably keep a journal that you will have to update consistently.

A lot of the work is done in the classroom with related studies, reflecting, reporting, and keeping accurate records, but that's up to your teacher.

Check the National Service-Learning Clearinghouse or the Corporation for National and Community Service online. They may have projects similar to what you have in mind with the suggested curriculum ties already listed. If projects for middle and high school are sparse, consider adapting one of the many projects in the higher learning categories. Or see if you can upgrade one of the elementary school projects. With the help of your teacher or counselor, you may need to adapt the project to your community's unique needs.

The class consensus may be that for now helping adults to become citizens is too big a project. Building trust may be the first step—the only step for this semester. Depending on the time you are willing to commit—a semester, a year, or in building blocks from freshman through senior years—your project may be as simple as getting two communities communicating or as complicated as preparing for the citizenship test. One project does not fit all.

FROM PASSION TO PROJECT

Some projects seem deceptively simple. On Giants' Shoulders is not the first or only "cyber buddy" project, but it seems to be one of the most successful. Dale defined it more by what it isn't than by what it is: "It is not tutoring, not homework help, and not a Big Brother/Big Sister type program." Instead, it matches interests of motivated advantaged older students

> ATTITUDE COUNTS, TOO

Besides time, what do you have in your personality and skill toolbox? If you are excited about the service, it will quickly spread to others.

Are you a people person? That is, do you have the knack to put people of all ages at ease? Remember, most people are eager to talk about themselves. Be more interested in them than in your role as volunteer. Have a list of possible questions to get the conversation started. Immigrants are from somewhere else. If you know that ahead of time, read up on where they're from so that you'll have better questions. For example, you discover that your subject is from a

Enthusiasm is contagious. Students who are excited about their project can inspire even the most reluctant or shy to participate. Reach out to classmates and others to explain the goals and needs of your project.

village of only three hundred people. That's probably fewer than the number of students in your school. Doesn't that raise a lot of questions in your mind?

Do you have the patience for repetition without showing boredom or disappointment? Expect to repeat and even lose ground sometimes. It's natural for most people. You learned words and their meanings gradually as a child, observing and trying them for yourself.

Are you good with younger kids? (If your counselor asked your sibling this question, would your answers agree?) Remember when you were that age, and don't compare them with who you are now.

"Remember," Lola (a pseudonym) said, "speaking a different language doesn't make you smarter or better. Maybe we know something you don't." She warned that starting with a superior attitude won't get you anywhere.

with those of less advantaged, at-risk younger kids. Through a few minutes chat each week via webcams, the high school students became role models.

The elementary students were motivated, learned communication skills, and were encouraged to respect their teachers, school, and the learning process while improving their computer skills. It didn't cost much, either. The involved schools already had web cameras and were connected to the Internet. Even so, it took thousands of e-mails to set it up, Dale said.

The high school students gained experience in leadership, responsibility, and developed a working partnership with the other school. The media coverage

With minimal technology—Internet, webcams, and programs like Skype—you can reach out to students in need at other schools. Even after a few minutes a week, you will see how much you can learn from each other.

nationally and locally (viewable on the website) gave a positive image to counter the often negative coverage of youth. The experience convinced Dale that she wanted to be a child psychologist.

The name, On Giants' Shoulders—derived from the words of Sir Isaac Newton—may have had something to do with their success, too. The name piques curiosity and opens the door for dialogue about the need for such programs.

When you name your own project, you might want to skip the generic title and call it something familiar like Rock Paper Scissors: rock for the wall that stands between the communities, paper for the documents you will help them earn, and scissors for cutting away the barriers, for instance. Think of a few key words and look them up in *Bartlett's Familiar Quotations* for inspiration. Find the right Spanish words if you aim to work with Spanish speakers—*amigos* ("friend") is a good start. Go from there.

CHAPTER THREE

PREP AND PLAN

The most successful projects happen when students, faculty, and the community are equal partners in shaping the experience. But consult a map before you start your trip. Mark where you are and where you want to be, and follow the path before you. You can find help on the web. Youth Service America has downloadable tool kits for your planning stage. Brown University in Providence, Rhode Island, put together a tool kit for colleges and universities participating in service learning. Although it is aimed at higher learning, it has points that can be adapted to middle- and high-school projects.

When your finance committee has priced supplies and added a 10 percent buffer for any surprises that may occur, it's time to use some creative thinking to find local funding. With luck, the organization that helps you with supplies may also be your community sponsor. Blending small grants may be necessary.

One of the projects tackled in the Los Angeles Unified School District, for instance, was on behalf of migrant farmworkers. After studying the Great

There are many service-learning opportunities that involve working with migrant farmers. These farmers usually spend long hours doing back-breaking work in the fields and are exposed to various health risks, such as those caused by exposure to pesticides.

Depression in social studies, the students researched problems migrant farmers face today. They discovered poor living conditions, exposure to pesticides, poor pay, and child labor.

The students wrote letters to government officials and legislators suggesting changes to the laws. They called on the United Farm Workers, Campaign for Children in the Field, and National Consumer League to be their community partners. You can download their project plan from the district's website and adapt it to your specific community situation.

That district's website also details a project to make a video, *Coming to America*, conducted by a junior social studies class that noted ethnic tensions on campus. With support from the Anti-Defamation League, Immigration and Customs Enforcement, Amnesty International, and diverse ethnic groups, they made a video that gave a better understanding of events that led to immigration. The purpose was to create tolerance between cultures and diminish tensions. Both projects have clear goals to correct recognized challenges. The sponsors all have a stake in those goals.

BREAKING THROUGH THE WALL OF DISTRUST

A good place to start when looking for a project is checking local newspapers and government websites for news about the migrant and immigrant challenges locally and nationally. The website Partnership for a New American Economy is another option. The site provides current statistics and future projections on immigration for each state.

Consult with your local government agencies and call for an information packet from organizations and associations connected to immigration or migration. They are more apt to be on top of the specific needs in your community. Once you have gathered the information, it is time to analyze it. To avoid duplication, find out what projects are ongoing in your area.

PERSUADING SPONSORS

Look at your own project. Who in your community will be interested enough to invest time and funds? Sponsors' responsibilities include at least a few meetings, periodic reports, signing off on the number of hours you contributed, and offering evaluations. They are investing more than their names in your project. Some may never have participated in service learning before. Or they may have had a bad experience in the past. You may have to convince them—invite them to your class during a brainstorming session.

Some projects, like creating a city or county history of immigration, may span several years and involve interviewing families, editing, and collating the stories into a cohesive history for the area library. It took a higher learning institution seven quarters to complete. How would you divide it into measurable steps? Will you need different sponsors for each step, or will your initial sponsor stay for the duration?

Create a persuasive presentation. Use photos, graphs, and an attractive layout. Keep it simple. In as few words as possible, state the community challenge, your project, and the impact you want to make.

In the next segment, state what you expect from the sponsor: expertise, liaison with the community, facilities, and funds.

Presenting your project and its potential for community impact is essential to securing the sponsors and funding you need. Effective visuals that summarize or complement important facts can be useful tools in your presentation.

Few projects are completely free to produce. Even if you can download manuals for free, you still need paper and ink to reproduce them for whatever number you work with. Your supply committee needs to anticipate everything from pencils, notepads, poster boards, and paints.

Funding is finite. National and local grants are in demand as more schools participate in service learning. You may need to find numerous donors just as the California students did. Consider the state and area history and genealogical societies as sponsors. See if local, state, or federal grants are available to your project. Check out your local phone directory under associations and organizations. Look at government department listings for departments that share your interest.

Your school probably has a newspaper and a yearbook. Those staffs have advertising sellers already practiced in convincing area businesses to invest in ads. Draft those go-getters to do the footwork for locals. Area libraries list their donors. It could take thousands of e-mails to produce only a few investors.

Look to local literacy organizations and ethnic associations for funding. For instance, the Edward Ginsberg Center for Community Service and Learning offers grants and space in southeast Michigan. The University of North Carolina Center for Public Service has grants for that area. National companies like AmeriCorps, IBM, Walmart, Disney Friends for Change, and State Farm are also possibilities.

In your local area, look to the businesses that could use some good public relations. An online or

> YOU NEED ONLY TO ASK

If there is no willing sponsor, how will you raise the funds: Saturday car wash? Bake sale? Used book sale? What businesses in your area are more likely to donate supplies for things like printing or reproducing posters? Browse the school paper and year-book for ads from the locals. Start by thanking them for their past support, and then tell them what you need. Remind them that they will be listed on your website and in publicity materials.

You may not even need a grant; check with the school custodian. Leftover supplies are stored at the end of the school year. What you need may be there for the taking.

Ask to put a list of needs on the bulletin board in the faculty lounge, on the school bulletin board, and in the morning announcements. Never underestimate the power of proud parents for donations and transportation.

Post your needs on every available bulletin board, but make sure that your ad has visual impact so that it stands out from the others.

Grocery stores have bulletin boards, and community newspapers may be willing to do articles on your cause or give you ad space.

Look on websites like Freecycle.org. You may get lucky and get that used laptop you need for free, or something else on your list.

local phone directory will have organizations listed. Many have websites with application forms.

TIMING IS EVERYTHING

Get out your calendar and circle every possible celebration day that relates to your project on immigration. National Hispanic Heritage Month is the period from September 15 to October 15 in the United States. It recognizes the contributions of Hispanic and Latino Americans to the United States and celebrates the group's heritage and culture. Cinco de Mayo (May 5) is a time of celebration in the United States by Mexican nationals and their descendants. How might you use the occasion to call attention to your project?

May is Asian Pacific American Heritage Month, and World Day for Cultural Diversity for Dialogue and Development is May 21. September 11 is the National Day of Service and Remembrance. World Day Against Child Labor is in June.

If you can't find an existing celebration, create one. Ask your principal to declare it a Salute to Hispanic Heritage Day in your school. If you thought far enough ahead about this, posters of declaration in every hallway can make it special. Ask the cafeteria to plan a special menu for that day. Publicity generates enthusiasm. Enthusiasm generates volunteers with fresh ideas. The more tie-ins you can come up with, the more successful your project will be. Draft the music, drama, and art departments to come up with their own contributions. You then have the perfect atmosphere to launch your project website.

BIENVENIDOS, WELCOME

Many classes set up web pages about their service-learning project. You can design web pages for free through several web services, such as WordPress. You can design your own or use one of their templates. You will want to launch your project's website as soon as you clarify your project goals; call for volunteers from outside your class to supplement with needed skills.

Select appropriate music now in the public domain, or perhaps you have a musician among your group who can create a song for your site. Write about your impending service-learning project and invite others to join you. Keep it fresh with frequent updates on progress, needs, and donors. Add an attractive logo and photos that you update frequently.

If you have your sponsor, keep that name prominent on the page. Explain your mutual goals. Now is the time to ask for volunteers. Make it like a classified: Opportunities Available. List the benefits: curriculum-based service learning, etc.

An attractive website will help your project get attention. Refer to it through Facebook and Twitter. Bright images and frequent updates keep viewers coming back.

If you are still looking for a sponsor, you might have a highlighted area that says "Sponsor Wanted." When you present your proposal to potential sponsors, show them your website or, better yet, show them a mock-up with their business logo inserted as an incentive.

MAKE YOUR OWN RECORD

An important part of service learning is reflection and celebration. Although they are the final steps, their roots begin with your first discussions and continue through every step throughout the project. Whether you use a computer or handwritten notes, you need a record of your observations with dates, times, meeting place, the names of attendees, and the discussed points. The journal is your personal take. But you will be expected to report periodically by essay or orally in class and to your sponsor.

Take photos throughout the project to post on your website. You will cull out the best for your project's end report. Make sure that everyone is identified and that their names are correct. It would be better to have someone from the photography class shoot the photos. Cell phone photos are fine for quick takes, but you will want your final report to look as professional as possible.

It's important for the individuals you work with, participating organization(s), school, and you to agree on the mission terms. Articulate your goal in a simple direct sentence. For example: "The advanced Spanish class will coach interested drivers for the written driver's test." Or, "Our American history class will prepare and distribute information to newspapers, radio, and television stations advocating reform in our immigration laws." By clearly stating your goal, you will remain on track.

CHAPTER FOUR

GOING PUBLIC

Whether you are going it alone on a project or as a team, how you present yourself to sponsors, organizations, and the individuals you work with is as important as your project. Nobody's expecting you in your Sunday best, but neatness does count. Know what you're going to say before you speak— even if you are only making a phone call at first. Why all the preparation when they necessarily won't see you? Attitude comes through your voice.

When you contact an organization, you will probably be speaking to a receptionist or office assistant the first time. But you are probably not the first student to appeal to the organization's sense of community spirit. There is only a finite amount of funds set aside for grants or donations or dealing with student spokes-persons during busy office hours. Be succinct. Be focused. Be enthusiastic, but not gushy. Believe in your project, and be natural. Respect their time.

A well-written e-mail may be the best start. Write and rewrite until you have all the information neces-sary for the recipient to understand your project in a

> ## PRACTICE AWAY THE GLITCHES

If you plan to call instead of starting out with an e-mail, write down what you want to say, including how you will identify yourself. Practice it until it sounds natural and not read. Expect the unexpected. You may have expected a direct line or it may be a switchboard. Know your contact. You will probably talk to a receptionist or secretary; that's fine. The following is an example:

"Hello, my name is Harry. I am a junior at Roger's High School. We believe that our community is safer when all drivers are licensed and insured. As a service-learning project, my Spanish class has trained to prepare unlicensed drivers in the written test. We hope that when you hear our plan you will want to work with us on the project. Is there a convenient time to speak with you about this?"

Your contact may suggest an in-person meeting or ask you to send the details via e-mail. Make sure that you have the proper e-mail address, phone extension, and name of your contact in addition to the time.

few brief sentences, and make sure you have answers for the following:

- Who you represent (yourself, class, or school)
- What service you offer

- Why the project is important to you
- A time you can discuss the details further

If you are meeting in person, be sure that you have transportation and directions to the potential sponsor's office. Dress neatly, be punctual, and be prepared with any information you might need. Anticipate potential questions so you can answer without hesitation.

Proper attire and prompt arrival go a long way toward showing a potential sponsor that you are serious and enthusiastic about your project. Know your material by heart so that you can answer questions without hesitation.

Be clear on exactly what you expect a sponsor to do (promote your cause or provide contacts, information, funds, or facilities). If you need financing, know what you need and the costs. Have a sheet prepared with the necessities and costs.

It is a good idea to have a reliable stand-in, just as prepared as you are, ready to step in if an emergency pops up at the last minute.

WHILE YOU WERE MEETING

Meanwhile, back at school, your class will have committees on logistics, publicity, fund-raising, supplies procurement, and someone to coordinate the volunteers. It is good to have a mental walk-through of any events you might plan to iron out any bugs. Coordinate with community leaders to see that there are no competing events on the dates you have set.

When you establish committees, you will want to match talents to the duties. Take a good look at yourself. What skills do you have? Are you able to see the project as a whole, break it down into parts, and delegate to others? Can you motivate? Consult with your counselor. Who procrastinates? Who generates creative ideas? Who is a

Forming an effective committee means matching skills to needs and motivating each person to do his or her job before a deadline. The committee chair must always be aware of potential procrastinators and problems.

self-starter? Who can you depend on to show up on time, be well-groomed and neatly dressed? These are the classmates you can depend on. These are the ones who will work well with the community. Your best friend is not always the best choice. The gregarious ones may be good cheerleaders, but are they ready to do the quiet, behind-the-scenes jobs?

Clearly determine the responsibilities of each committee, including the frequency of updated reports. The logistics committee will investigate venues where your clients will be comfortable. Is there a community center or a church fellowship hall you can use? If it is a small group, libraries might have community rooms available to you. Do you need only chairs or tables? Who will set them up before the meeting, and who is responsible for storing them afterward? Will you need a computer or tablet, overhead projector and screen, and a sound system? Do you have printed matter for each attendee? These are the types of details you and your class or team will need to work through as you develop your project.

GET THE MEDIA INVOLVED EARLY

The promotion committee will see that public radio and television stations and both city-wide and community newspapers have hard copies detailing the important who, what, when where, why, and how of your project. On all publicity, provide contact information including a name, telephone number, and website address.

For broadcasts, time the broadcast information to be read in thirty seconds. If there are unfamiliar words, follow them with a phonetic pronunciation in parentheses. For newspapers, keep your ad or announcement brief with the most important information first. Send the first releases a month before the first event. Follow up by sending a second release with updated information a week before.

Most newspapers have a special school reporter. If not, check the local columnists, who are on the constant lookout for subjects. Think about how your project might fit into their format. Offer to arrange interviews with students. You will want to save resulting clippings and notations about broadcasts in your journal.

WALK IT OFF

If you host an informational event for the public, you will want to mentally walk through the event as if you are an attendee. What will they need? Make a checklist.

Do you need a greeter to direct them to the correct room?

Are you providing refreshments? That means offering choices and the appropriate utensils and dishware.

What about babysitters? If the project doesn't involve children, if space is limited, or the location prohibits small children, make it clear from the start that there will be no child care on the premises.

If you are using a facility that you are unfamiliar with, visit and walk through it to locate bathrooms, which doors will be available, and where the parking lot and nearest bus stops are. Discover safety concerns early. If you can't work around them, anticipate any problems the logistics may bring up and determine how to solve them.

CHECKING IT TWICE

As soon as you confirm the date of the first event, invite your sponsor and perhaps even someone familiar to the community and well respected as a guest speaker. Be specific about the time limit. Keep your own greeting brief. If you have a guest speaker, make sure to call a week before the event, and then on the day of, to confirm that he or she will be appearing. Make sure someone can greet, escort, and provide refreshments to the speaker as needed.

If you received donations like refreshments, printed materials, pencils and pads for each attendee, be sure that you have enough for everyone.

Assign several students to take photos of the event. Decide early if you will want random or specifically identified people. Instruct them to ask first if someone wants to be in a photograph. Respect their wishes. Know how you will use them: on your website, for the school paper, to document your project, to donate to the local community center, or something else?

Briefly thank all volunteers, sponsors, special guests. Thank those who came, and if this is to be an ongoing project, remind them when the next meeting will be.

When selecting your program speakers, keep community leaders in mind. The target clients might already know them, and they will attract a few people who might not otherwise come.

THE LONG AND THE SHORT OF IT

You need a specific time frame that you and those you work with will have to agree on. Will it be two hours alternate Friday evenings? Is it three hours on two Saturday mornings? Begin and end on time. And clean the facility and return it to normal, if necessary. Collect any unused materials for later use.

If you're working with a group of people, don't be discouraged if fewer people attend the later meetings. Keep your focus on your goal. Show as much enthusiasm for the dwindling crowd as you did for the first event. Perhaps you feel that next time you will need to have better incentives to attract them again.

KEEPING THE RECORD STRAIGHT

How you approach those you work with will shape your success. You need to build trust and be a good listener, especially for one-on-one interactions. For example, if you want to interview older citizens at senior centers or community centers, who may enjoy talking about their family history and transcribe what they said, you will want to have questions ready that will prompt their memories. Do they have older or younger siblings? What was a typical day like? How did they celebrate holidays?

Senior centers are rich with older people who enjoy sharing family stories—often from their country of origin—and photo albums. Helping them to chronicle their memories is a service to them and to community libraries.

Don't interrupt, but wait and ask questions about something they said. Repeat back to them in your own words what they said. It validates your interest. What did they bring with them? Did they bring photos? Do they have a photo album? Photos trigger memories. Foods act as triggers, too. Perhaps for your second meeting you can arrange to bring something that they mentioned. You might bring photos of your family. When they mention their town of birth, make a point to look it up and find out what you can about it to mention the next time you speak.

Perhaps you decide on an indirect service like providing information to the public through the media or petitioning your local representative to work on a bill to protect the farmworkers from the hazardous, sometimes lethal, pesticides. Will you work to make a law that employers must provide protective gear like gloves and face masks and proper areas to clean up before the workers carry the dangers to their family?

Will you work with local clinics to get information on the pesticides used in your area? The workers are predominantly Latino, but many are Asian and Pacific Islanders. A class visit to a local farm may be an eye-opener. Essays, interviews (if they are willing), letters to the editor, and articles on the school pages all bring awareness. Workers, especially the undocumented, may be afraid to speak up. Your decision to be their voice is a worthy service-learning project. By putting a face on a situation, you challenge others to join you in a solution.

CHAPTER FIVE

REFLECT AND CELEBRATE

As your classes come to an end, one of the most important celebrations will be the close of your service-learning project and a job well done. You spent a semester, perhaps more, studying the community, planning, and taking action. But you are not quite through with your project.

Reflection not only helps you to look at the project as a whole, but also aids you in offering insights as to how it can be improved in the future. You will set your emotions aside for now and evaluate each step for its strengths or any weaknesses. Reflection allows you to forge a path for others to follow.

START AT THE BEGINNING

While your actual assignments will vary by class, your teachers will very likely ask you to write about your experiences during service learning in some form and present them once your project has been completed. This would be the time to spin your story of discovery for those who may follow in your footsteps. And it is

Inspiration for a service-learning project may come from a passage in your social studies textbook, breaking news in the media, or a novel that tugs at your sense of social justice.

a story, so start from the beginning. What were you studying in class at the time? Was it a textbook, something a classmate said, or perhaps a news story that related to the subject?

Did you start a discussion with a few friends, or did you ask for a class discussion about how you might help? Explain the research you did before you approached your classmates. Did you check the national clearinghouse and your school district for projects that had been completed already? If so, were you able to contact the previous leader for updates and suggestions?

BACK TO THE FUTURE

The reflection period is also the time to sort and organize all those notes and observations you made throughout the project. You wrote down your goal and how you might achieve it. Looking back, was it a realistic goal? How did you persuade your classmates that your project was a good idea? Include the positive and negative comments. Discuss how you found a sponsor.

Add your thoughts about the early steps, and if you had any initial doubts and how you overcame them. You may have adjusted your expectations at some point. Relate how they changed and why. What do you consider a success in such a project? Your narrative should be an honest appraisal.

Some other questions to consider as you reflect could be: What do you feel you learned in your service-learning project? Did you feel more comfortable in a leadership role? Do you think that will help you to succeed in college? What did you discover about yourself that you hadn't realized before? What about your service did you feel were most satisfying to you? Has your perception of the community you worked with changed?

Discuss with your teammates or classmates what they learned and how they felt. Compare your reactions and see if you can think of ways the project could be improved in the future or how you might use what you gained in your future pursuits.

At the end of your project, you will present a roundup exploring how well you met your goals. It is a time for honest evaluation, listing any problems you encountered as well as your successes.

A MEASURE OF SUCCESS

How can you measure the success? By attendance? By participation? By the comments? (Did you ask for the participants' comments at the end?) Did you help them feel good about themselves?

Part of your sponsor's contract with you is to give you feedback at the end of the service. How did you perform by their standards?

List the skills you learned in the project: leadership, organization, appreciation of others' talents and teamwork, for instance. You probably honed your skills in inspiring others, as well as gaining an ability to communicate more comfortably with other cultures and generations. You analyzed facts instead of relying on rhetoric, etc. Explain how you can apply these skills in your other academic pursuits and in your everyday life.

While there is no one measure of success, your greatest takeaway should be a feeling of mutual gain between yourself and the community you worked with. Consider how much you think relations between the immigrant community and yours has changed for the better.

With everything you gathered fed into your computer, you will be able to organize and integrate all feedback into the final presentation. It will become a model for future classes to follow, a resource for the sponsor, and a demonstration to your teacher(s) the extent of the service you performed and what you learned from it. It will include not only what you did and when, but also your impressions of how well it all fit into the curricula. Include copies of any letters you wrote and received.

SHOULD OTHERS GIVE IT A TRY?

Do you believe others will benefit from working with the sponsor agency in the future? Present your reflection without judgment or complaint. Let the facts speak for themselves. Make suggestions on how the school or an individual might follow up on the project. What more can be done?

When your project ends, you will report on it to your class, listing the skills you learned and discussing how your work corresponded to your curriculum.

Do you feel that your sponsor(s) offered enough supervision, support, and public enthusiasm? Was the sponsor forthcoming with periodic feedback? Do you feel that they fairly evaluated your performance and the project?

Don't forget to show how you used math (calculating the funds needed), communication, English, language, and skills from any other classes that might have tied into your project.

Don't be afraid to list diverse opinions you received. Not everyone thinks or reacts in the same way. Do you feel that the project is worth repeating by you or by someone else? If so, do you have any suggestions for improvement?

SHARING THE GOOD NEWS

Celebration through recognition and publicizing your project is an important part of the project. Written essays, art, speeches to other classes, school assemblies, the school board, and to the town hall or open city council meetings bring attention to your school and project outside of the classroom.

Turn your website into a celebration. Organize any photos and testimonials, and use the space to publicly thank all of the volunteers—donors and sponsors—who helped make it possible. Keep the contact information updated. You may find, like On Giants' Shoulders, Mix It Up, and other successful projects, that others may need to ask advice. Get creative with hashtags to create traffic. Keep

> HOW EFFECTIVE WERE YOU?

If you worked alone on a project in partnership with a nonprofit agency, you will need them to evaluate your participation before you receive credit. They will need to report the following:

Did you live up to the full agreement of your duties and responsibilities? Before you began, the two of you discussed the need, expectations, and challenges. Did you overestimate your goals for the time allowed? If during the service you became aware that it was more difficult to perform than you felt capable, did you consult with your sponsor and teacher?

A good practice is to make mini-evaluations as you work through your service. Your sponsor should consult with you periodically so that you know where you stand. If you felt overwhelmed at any time, did you tell them?

Were you professional in your appearance and performance with the staff? You might in the beginning ask your sponsor what is considered appropriate attire for the location. Did you appear motivated to do your best at all times?

Were you trusted to work without supervision the entire time? Were you always on time, and if you could not keep a regular appointment, did you call to say so ahead of time? Did you mislead them on your abilities in any way?

Ask your sponsor(s) for suggestions on improvement in the future. Their feedback is essential to not only your grade but also to those future students who will want to follow in your footsteps.

a counter on your website so that you can measure the number of visitors. Add a place for comments.

Create a video or a scrapbook. Display it online or In the central library or on a traveling display throughout the school district. Involve the community papers, which will give you more coverage than the city paper. Prepare press releases.

Don't forget to thank everyone. Write a thank-you note that is unique to each volunteer, naming what they did or how many hours they gave for the cause. If you used facilities free of charge, write the owner. Leave no one out.

Share your project with the National Service-Learning Clearinghouse

Remember that you didn't do your project alone. Don't forget to write personal thank-you notes to volunteers, sponsors, and donors. Mention their specific contributions.

and the Youth Service America. See if it is possible to present each volunteer a thank-you for his or her participation in the project, naming the recorded hours and specific committee.

Youth Service America certifies for the President's Volunteer Service Award. You can follow their guidelines for submitting your project to see if yours qualifies.

The next time someone says, "You're just kids. What can you do?" you will have the answer. When you, your classmates, teachers, and community work together the answer is: a lot.

You have already mastered the tools of change and can coax information from computers and pass it forward in a nanosecond. Add a strong sense of social justice, and you can move others to action. Using social media, you will mark a path for future service learners with a permanent record of your achievement.

Remember, though, that your gains are not measured in plaques for your wall or in letters of recommendation. The true measure is that you made a difference in your community and proved to all that you are ready for the responsibilities and the privileges you will soon claim as your own.

GLOSSARY

advocacy The act of publicly supporting something, such as an idea, cause, individual, or policy.

budgeting Calculating a reasonable amount of money to spend for a specific purpose by factoring in available resources and various costs.

community A group of people bound together by a physical area or a common interest.

cultural Of or relating to ethnic, racial, social, traditional, or ethnic similarities, as in people from a similar background.

deferred Delayed until a later time.

deportation The physical removal of a foreign-born resident from a country, usually to the individual's country of origin.

diversity A wide range of items together; often in reference to different ethnic or minority groups in a single location or region.

documented Describing an immigrant who has entered a country with papers indicating his or her legal right to be there.

Dreamer A person of a certain age brought as a child to the United States by parents who entered illegally.

family tree A document tracking one's ancestors from the past to the present generation.

green card A document given to a foreign-born individual that allows him or her to legally reside and work in a country for an extended period of time.

guest worker One who holds a visa with permission to work for a limited time period.

immigrant A person who lives in a country not of his birth; a foreign-born resident.

migrant One who moves about the country and takes temporary work, such as planting and harvesting produce on farms.

naturalization The legal process that an immigrant or non-citizen resident goes through to become a citizen of a particular country.

persecution The cruel or unfair treatment of someone, often because of his or her religious or political beliefs.

pesticide A chemical that kills insects or other organisms that destroy or harm plants or crops.

refugee Someone who fled or was forced to leave a country, often because of war, violence, religious or political reasons, or some other form or persecution.

sponsor An organization, business, or individual that agrees to assist through expertise, guidance, and funding.

visa A document that allows a foreign-born individual to enter a country.

FOR MORE INFORMATION

Canadian Alliance for Community Service-Learning
2128 Dunton Tower
Carleton University
1125 Colonel By Drive
Ottawa, ON K1S 5B6
Canada
(613) 520-2600
Website: http://www.communityservicelearning.ca/en
The Canadian Alliance for Community Service-Learning
   works to bring together students, educators, and
   members of the community to help service learning
   develop throughout Canada.

Corporation for National and Community Service
1201 New York Avenue NW
Washington, DC 20525
(202) 606-5000
Website: http://www.nationalservice.gov
The Corporation for National and Community Service
   comprises AmeriCorps, Senior Corps, the Social
   Innovation Fund, the Volunteer Generation Fund,
   and more. It partners with local organizations to
   address a number of issues facing the United
   States and to improve the lives of individuals
   around the country.

Imagining America
203 Tolley Building
Syracuse University
Syracuse, NY 13244
(315) 443-8590

Website: http://imaginingamerica.org
Imagining America brings together artists, scholars, members of the community, and others to contribute to community action and civic life.

The J.W. McConnell Family Foundation
Suite 1800
1002 Sherbrooke Street West
Montreal, QC H3A 3L6
Canada
(514) 288-2133
Website: http://www.mcconnellfoundation.ca/en
The J.W. McConnell Family Foundation is a private philanthropic organization funding programs that support public life and help build sustainable communities.

National Service-Learning Partnership
Website: http://www.service-learningpartnership.org
The National Service-learning Partnership is committed to integrating service learning as a central part of every young person's education.

National Youth Leadership Council
1667 Snelling Avenue North, Suite D300
Saint Paul, MN 55108
(651) 631-3672
Website: http://www.nylc.org
The National Youth Leadership Council supports educators, students, and communities by providing high quality, dynamic, service-learning content that align with curricula to school districts.

Refugee & Immigrant Assistance Center (RIAC)
31 Heath St.
Jamaica Plain, MA 02130
(617) 238-2430
Website: http://www.riacboston.org
RIAC supports refugees, asylees, and immigrants and
    promotes their successful resettlment by providing
    services such as counseling, education, outreach,
    and more.

United Farm Workers
National Headquarters
P.O. Box 62
29700 Woodford-Tehachapi Road
Keene, CA 93531
(661) 823-6151
Website: http://www.ufw.org
The United Farm Workers of America is the nation's
    largest farm workers union and is currently active
    in ten states.

WEBSITES

Because of the changing nature of Internet links, Rosen
Publishing has developed an online list of websites
related to the subject of this book. This site is updated
regularly. Please use this link to access the list:

http://www.rosenlinks.com/SLFT/Immi

FOR FURTHER READING

Alvarez, Julia. *Return to Sender.* New York, NY: Yearling Books, 2010.

Angotti, Tom, Cheryl S. Doble, and Paula Horrigan. *Service Learning in Design and Planning: Educating at the Boundaries.* Oakland, CA: New Village Press, 2012.

Bausum, Ann. *Denied, Detained, Deported: Stories from the Dark Side of American Immigration.* Des Moines, IA: National Geographic, 2009.

Bourgois, Philippe. *Fresh Fruit, Broken Bodies: Migrant Farmworkers in the United States.* Berkeley, CA: University of California Press, 2013.

Bush, Jeb, and Clint Bolick. *Immigration Wars: Forging an American Solution.* New York, NY: Threshold Editions, 2014.

Butin, Dan W. *Service-Learning in Theory and Practice: The Future of Community Engagement in Higher Learning.* New York, NY: Palgrave Macmillan, 2010.

Cipolle, Susan Benigni. *Service-Learning and Social Justice: Engaging Students in Social Change.* Lanham, MD: Rowman and Littlefield, Inc., 2010.

Duncan, Joyce, and Teresa Brooks Taylor. *Coming Full Circle: A Guide to Service Learning.* San Diego, CA: Cognella Academic Publishing, 2012.

Friedman, Jenny, and Jolene Rochlkepartain. *Doing Good Together: 101 Easy, Meaningful Service Projects for Families, Schools, and Communities.* Minneapolis, MN: Free Spirit Publishing, 2010.

Ghadar, Fairborz. *Becoming American: Why Immigration is Good for Our Nation's Future.* Lanham, MD: Rowman and Littlefield, Inc., 2014.

Hatcher, Julie, and Robert G. Bringle. *Understanding Service-Learning and Community Engagement: Crossing Boundaries through Research.* Charlotte, NC: Information Age Publishing, Inc., 2011.

Hickman, Pamela. *Righting Canada's Wrongs: The Komagata Maru and Canada's Anti-Indian Immigration Policies in the Twentieth Century.* Toronto, Canada: James Lorimer & Company, Ltd., 2014.

Kinloch, Valerie, and Peter Smagorinsky. *Service-Learning in Literacy Education: Possibilities for Teaching and Learning.* Charlotte, NC: Information Age Publishing, Inc., 2014.

Nazario, Sonia. *Enrique's Journey: The True Story of a Boy Determined to Reunite with His Mother.* New York, NY: Delacorte Books for Young Readers, 2013.

Para Pinto, Alejandro, and Alvaro Parra Pinto. *Children's Books in Easy Spanish 5: Sirenita (Intermediate Level): Spanish Readers for Kids of All Ages.* Caracas, Venezuela: Ediciones De La Parra, 2014.

Robinson, Jerry W., and Guy P. Green. *Introduction to Community Development: Theory, Practice, and Service-Learning.* Thousand Oaks, CA: SAGE Publications, 2010.

Schrover, Marlou, and Willem Schinkel. *The Language of Inclusion and Exclusion in Immigration and Integration* (Ethnic and Racial Studies). England: Taylor and Francis, 2014.

Schwab, William A., and David Gearhart. *Right to Dream: Immigration Reform and America's Future.* Fayetteville, Arkansas: University of Arkansas Press, 2013.

Stoeker, Randy, and Elizabeth Tryon. *The Unheard Voices: Community Organizations and Service Learning.* Philadelphia: Temple University Press, 2009.

Varona, Lucia T., and Carmen Chaves Tessner. *Construyendo Puentes (Building Bridges): Concepts and Models for Service-Learning in Spanish.* Sterling, VA: Stylus Publishing, LLC, 1999.

BIBLIOGRAPHY

Associated Press with KPCC Staff. "Gov. Brown signs 'Trust Act' prohibiting detaining undocumented for deportation in minor arrests." Southern California Public Radio, October 5, 2013. Retrieved December 6, 2013 (http://www.scpr.org/news/2013/10/05/39668/california-gov-jerry-brown-signs-trust-act-into-la).

Beadle, Amanda Peterson. "From the Mouths of Babes: Children Demand Immigration Reform." Retrieved December 6, 2013 (http://immigrationimpact.com/2013/12/06/from-the-mouths-of-babes-children-demand-immigration-reform).

Benson, Peter. *Tobacco Capitalism: Growers, Migrant Workers, and the Changing Face of a Global Industry.* Princeton, NJ: Princeton University Press, 2011.

Caraballo, Edda "Binational Migrant Education Program." California Department of Education. Retrieved February 6, 2014 (http://www.cde.ca.gov/sp/me/il/binational.asp).

Caraballo, Edda. "Migrant Education Programs and Services." Retrieved February 6, 2014 (http://www.cde.ca.gov/sp/me/mt/programs.asp).

Dale, Chelsea. "On Giants' Shoulders." Retrieved December 19, 2013 (http://www.ongiantsshoulders.org).

Denier, Nicole, and Joey Hoffman. "English as Second Language Homework Club." Retrieved February 21, 2014 (http://www.marylandpublicschools.org/MSDE/programs/servicelearning/docs/archive/sherry_unger/2005_02_01.htm).

Department of Homeland Security. "Other Ways to Get a Green Card." Retrieved January 30, 2014 (http://www.dhs.gov/how-do-i/get-green-card). Washington, D.C.

Familias Inmigrantes y Estudtantes en la Lucha/ Immigrant Families and Students in the Struggle. Retrieved February 14, 2014 (www.fielhouston.org).

Farber, Katy. *How to Create, Lead, and Assess Service Learning.* Lanham, MD: Rowman and Littlefield Education, 2011.

Farber, Katy. *Change the World with Service Learning: How to Organize, Lead, and Assess Service-Learning Projects.* Lanham, MD: Rowman & Littlefield Education, 2013.

Guggenheim, Davis, film director. *The Dream is Now,* 2013. Retrieved February 14, 2014 (http://www.thedreamisnow.org).

Isaacson, Rick, and Jeff Saperstein. *The Art and Strategy of Service-Learning Presentations.* Toronto, Ontario, Canada: Cengage Learning, 2005.

Kaye, Cathryn Berger. *The Complete Guide to Service Learning: Proven Practical Ways to Engage Students in Civic Responsibility, Academic Curriculum, & Social Action.* Minneapolis, MN: Free Spirit, 2013.

Leingang, Rachel. "Canada Provides Housing for Migrant Workers; in US Most Must Find Their Own." Two Borders. Retrieved January 20, 2014 (http://cronkite.asu.edu/buffett/canada/workerhousing.html).

Lewis, Barbara A. *The Kid's Guide to Service Projects: Over 500 Service Ideas for Young People Who Want to Make a Difference.* Minneapolis, MN: Free Spirit, Rev. 2009.

Migrant Clinicians' Network. "The Migrant/Seasonal Farmworker." NPR, July 4, 2010. Retrieved December 19, 2013 (http://www.migrantclinician.org).

NPR Staff. "A Reagan Legacy: Amnesty for Illegal Aliens." Retrieved December 19, 2013 (http://www.npr.org/templates/story/story.php?storyId=128303672).

U.S. Citizenship and Immigration Services. "Helping Immigrants Become New Americans: Communities Discuss the Issues." Retrieved February 14, 2014 (http://www.uscis.gov/sites/default/files/files/article/focusgroup.pdf).

U.S. Department of Agriculture. "The Potential Impact of Changes in Immigration Policy on U.S. Agriculture and the Market for Hired Farm Labor: A Simulation Analysis." May 2012. Retrieved December 19, 2013 (http://ers.usda.gov/publications/err-economic-research-report/err135.aspx#.U2fb5MajTfM).

Zahniser, Stephen, Thomas Hertz, Maureen Rimmer and Peter Dixon, USDA, Economic Research Service, "The Potential Impact of Changes in Immigration Policy on U.S. Agriculture and the Market for Hired Farm Labor: A Simulation Analysis."

INDEX

ABOUT THE AUTHOR

Mary Blount Christian graduated from the University of Houston with a degree in journalism and worked as a reporter for *The Houston Post* before retiring to write more than one hundred fiction and non-fiction books for children and adults. She became interested in immigration while tracing her family tree. She taught creative writing at Houston Community College, on the local PBS station KHTV in Houston, and at Rice University's School of Continuing Studies.

PHOTO CREDITS

Cover The Washington Post/Getty Images; p. 3 bymandesigns/Shutterstock .com; pp. 4–5 Dean Mitchell/E+/Getty Images; p. 8 FuzzBones/Shutterstock .com; pp. 10–11 michaeljung/Shutterstock.com; p. 13 Fuse/Getty Images; p. 14 Image Source/Getty Images; p. 17 John Moore/Getty Images; p. 20 Tom Williams/CQ-Roll Call Group/Getty Images; p. 22 © iStockphoto.com/ eurobanks; p. 24 Jamie Grill/The Image Bank/Getty Images; p. 27 Monkey Business Images/Shutterstock.com; p. 30 Jon Feingersh/Blend Images/ Getty Images; p. 32 Ariel Skelley/Blend Images/Getty Images; 34 Flashon Studio/Shutterstock.com; p. 35 Education Images/Universal Images Group/ Getty Images; p. 38 Klaus Tiedge/Blend Images/Getty Images; p. 40 Maskot/Getty Images; p. 43 Stephen Coburn/Shutterstock.com; p. 45 Antonio Guillem/Shutterstock.com; p. 47 Nick White and Fiona Jackson-Downes/Cultura/Getty Images; pp. 48–49 Ridofranz/iStock/Thinkstock; p. 53 Alina Solovyova-Vincent/E+/Getty Images; p. 55 © iStockphoto. com/1MoreCreative; p. 57 Tom Wang/Shutterstock.com; pp. 58–59 sturti/ Vetta/Getty Images; p. 60 Chris Schmidt/E+/Getty Images; p. 62 Image Source/Getty Images; p. 65 LWA/Dann Tardif/Blend Images/Getty Images; cover and interior pages background textures and patterns vector illustration/ Shutterstock.com, Apostrophe/Shutterstock.com, nattanan726/Shutterstock .com, Yulia Glam/Shutterstock.com; back cover silhouette Pavel L Photo and Video/Shutterstock.com.

Designer: Michael Moy; Editor: Shalini Saxena;
Photo Researcher: Karen Huang